# LAYERS OF LEARNING

## YEAR ONE • UNIT TWELVE

ARABIA

RIVERS & LAKES

ATOMS

COLOR & VALUE

HooDoo Publishing
United States of America
©2014 Layers of Learning
Copies of maps or activities may be made for a particular family or classroom.
ISBN 978-1494943967

# Units At A Glance: Topics For All Four Years of the Layers of Learning Program

| 1 | History | Geography | Science | The Arts |
|---|---------|-----------|---------|----------|
| 1 | Mesopotamia | Maps & Globes | Planets | Cave Paintings |
| 2 | Egypt | Map Keys | Stars | Egyptian Art |
| 3 | Europe | Global Grids | Earth & Moon | Crafts |
| 4 | Ancient Greece | Wonders | Satellites | Greek Art |
| 5 | Babylon | Mapping People | Humans in Space | Poetry |
| 6 | The Levant | Physical Earth | Laws of Motion | List Poems |
| 7 | Phoenicians | Oceans | Motion | Moral Stories |
| 8 | Assyrians | Deserts | Fluids | Rhythm |
| 9 | Persians | Arctic | Waves | Melody |
| 10 | Ancient China | Forests | Machines | Chinese Art |
| 11 | Early Japan | Mountains | States of Matter | Line & Shape |
| 12 | Arabia | Rivers & Lakes | Atoms | Color & Value |
| 13 | Ancient India | Grasslands | Elements | Texture & Form |
| 14 | Ancient Africa | Africa | Bonding | African Tales |
| 15 | First North Americans | North America | Salts | Creative Kids |
| 16 | Ancient South America | South America | Plants | South American Art |
| 17 | Celts | Europe | Flowering Plants | Jewelry |
| 18 | Roman Republic | Asia | Trees | Roman Art |
| 19 | Christianity | Australia & Oceania | Simple Plants | Instruments |
| 20 | Roman Empire | You Explore | Fungi | Composing Music |

| 2 | History | Geography | Science | The Arts |
|---|---------|-----------|---------|----------|
| 1 | Byzantines | Turkey | Climate & Seasons | Byzantine Art |
| 2 | Barbarians | Ireland | Forecasting | Illumination |
| 3 | Islam | Arabian Peninsula | Clouds & Precipitation | Creative Kids |
| 4 | Vikings | Norway | Special Effects | Viking Art |
| 5 | Anglo Saxons | Britain | Wild Weather | King Arthur Tales |
| 6 | Charlemagne | France | Cells and DNA | Carolingian Art |
| 7 | Normans | Nigeria | Skeletons | Canterbury Tales |
| 8 | Feudal System | Germany | Muscles, Skin, & Cardiopulmonary | Gothic Art |
| 9 | Crusades | Balkans | Digestive & Senses | Religious Art |
| 10 | Burgundy, Venice, Spain | Switzerland | Nerves | Oil Paints |
| 11 | Wars of the Roses | Russia | Health | Minstrels & Plays |
| 12 | Eastern Europe | Hungary | Metals | Printmaking |
| 13 | African Kingdoms | Mali | Carbon Chem | Textiles |
| 14 | Asian Kingdoms | Southeast Asia | Non-metals | Vivid Language |
| 15 | Mongols | Caucasus | Gases | Fun With Poetry |
| 16 | Medieval China & Japan | China | Electricity | Asian Arts |
| 17 | Pacific Peoples | Micronesia | Circuits | Arts of the Islands |
| 18 | American Peoples | Canada | Technology | Indian Legends |
| 19 | The Renaissance | Italy | Magnetism | Renaissance Art I |
| 20 | Explorers | Caribbean Sea | Motors | Renaissance Art II |

| 3 | History | Geography | Science | The Arts |
|---|---|---|---|---|
| 1 | Age of Exploration | Argentina and Chile | Classification & Insects | Fairy Tales |
| 2 | The Ottoman Empire | Egypt and Libya | Reptiles & Amphibians | Poetry |
| 3 | Mogul Empire | Pakistan & Afghanistan | Fish | Mogul Arts |
| 4 | Reformation | Angola & Zambia | Birds | Reformation Art |
| 5 | Renaissance England | Tanzania & Kenya | Mammals & Primates | Shakespeare |
| 6 | Thirty Years' War | Spain | Sound | Baroque Music |
| 7 | The Dutch | Netherlands | Light & Optics | Baroque Art I |
| 8 | France | Indonesia | Bending Light | Baroque Art II |
| 9 | The Enlightenment | Korean Pen. | Color | Art Journaling |
| 10 | Russia & Prussia | Central Asia | History of Science | Watercolors |
| 11 | Conquistadors | Baltic States | Igneous Rocks | Creative Kids |
| 12 | Settlers | Peru & Bolivia | Sedimentary Rocks | Native American Art |
| 13 | 13 Colonies | Central America | Metamorphic Rocks | Settler Sayings |
| 14 | Slave Trade | Brazil | Gems & Minerals | Colonial Art |
| 15 | The South Pacific | Australasia | Fossils | Principles of Art |
| 16 | The British in India | India | Chemical Reactions | Classical Music |
| 17 | Boston Tea Party | Japan | Reversible Reactions | Folk Music |
| 18 | Founding Fathers | Iran | Compounds & Solutions | Rococo |
| 19 | Declaring Independence | Samoa and Tonga | Oxidation & Reduction | Creative Crafts I |
| 20 | The American Revolution | South Africa | Acids & Bases | Creative Crafts II |

| 4 | History | Geography | Science | The Arts |
|---|---|---|---|---|
| 1 | American Government | USA | Heat & Temperature | Patriotic Music |
| 2 | Expanding Nation | Pacific States | Motors & Engines | Tall Tales |
| 3 | Industrial Revolution | U.S. Landscapes | Energy | Romantic Art I |
| 4 | Revolutions | Mountain West States | Energy Sources | Romantic Art II |
| 5 | Africa | U.S. Political Maps | Energy Conversion | Impressionism I |
| 6 | The West | Southwest States | Earth Structure | Impressionism II |
| 7 | Civil War | National Parks | Plate Tectonics | Post-Impressionism |
| 8 | World War I | Plains States | Earthquakes | Expressionism |
| 9 | Totalitarianism | U.S. Economics | Volcanoes | Abstract Art |
| 10 | Great Depression | Heartland States | Mountain Building | Kinds of Art |
| 11 | World War II | Symbols and Landmarks | Chemistry of Air & Water | War Art |
| 12 | Modern East Asia | The South States | Food Chemistry | Modern Art |
| 13 | India's Independence | People of America | Industry | Pop Art |
| 14 | Israel | Appalachian States | Chemistry of Farming | Modern Music |
| 15 | Cold War | U.S. Territories | Chemistry of Medicine | Free Verse |
| 16 | Vietnam War | Atlantic States | Food Chains | Photography |
| 17 | Latin America | New England States | Animal Groups | Latin American Art |
| 18 | Civil Rights | Home State Study | Instincts | Theater & Film |
| 19 | Technology | Home State Study II | Habitats | Architecture |
| 20 | Terrorism | America in Review | Conservation | Creative Kids |

# Unit 1-12

## Printable Pack

This unit includes printables at the end. To make life easier for you we also created digital printable packs for each unit. To retrieve your printable pack for Unit 1-12, please visit

www.layers-of-learning.com/digital-printable-packs/

Put the printable pack in your shopping cart and use this coupon code:

**0107UNIT1-12**

Your printable pack will be free.

# LAYERS OF LEARNING INTRODUCTION

This is part of a series of units in the Layers of Learning homeschool curriculum, including the subjects of history, geography, science, and the arts. Children from 1st through 12th can participate in the same curriculum at the same time -family school style.

The units are intended to be used in order as the basis of a complete curriculum (once you add in a systematic math, reading, and writing program). You begin with Year 1 Unit 1 no matter what ages your children are. Spend about 2 weeks on each unit. You pick and choose the activities within the unit that appeal to you and read the books from the book list that are available to you or find others on the same topic from your library. We highly recommend that you use the timeline in every history section as the backbone. Then flesh out your learning with reading and activities that highlight the topics you think are the most important.

Alternatively, you can use the units as activity ideas to supplement another curriculum in any order you wish. You can still use them with all ages of children at the same time.

When you've finished with Year One, move on to Year Two, Year Three, and Year Four. Then begin again with Year One and work your way through the years again. Now your children will be older, reading more involved books, and writing more in depth. When you have completed the sequence for the second time, you start again on it for the third and final time. If your student began with Layers of Learning in 1st grade and stayed with it all the way through she would go through the four year rotation three times, firmly cementing the information in her mind in ever increasing depth. At each level you should expect increasing amounts of outside reading and writing. High schoolers in particular should be reading extensively, and if possible, participating in discussion groups.

☺ ☻ ☻ These icons will guide you in spotting activities and books that are appropriate for the age of child you are working with. But if you think an activity is too juvenile or too difficult for your kids, adjust accordingly. The icons are not there as rules, just guides.

☺ GRADES 1-4
☻ GRADES 5-8
☻ GRADES 9-12

Within each unit we share:
- EXPLORATIONS, activities relating to the topic;
- EXPERIMENTS, usually associated with science topics;
- EXPEDITIONS, field trips;
- EXPLANATIONS, teacher helps or educational philosophies.

In the sidebars we also include Additional Layers, Famous Folks, Fabulous Facts, On the Web, and other extra related topics that can take you off on tangents, exploring the world and your interests with a bit more freedom. The curriculum will always be there to pull you back on track when you're ready.

You can learn more about how to use this curriculum at www.layers-of-learning.com/layers-of-learning-program/

# UNIT TWELVE
## ARABIA – RIVERS & LAKES – ATOMS – COLOR & VALUE

*You may have tangible wealth untold;*
*Caskets of jewels and coffers of gold,*
*Richer than I you never can be--*
*I had a mother who read to me,.*
-Strickland Gillian

| | **LIBRARY LIST:** |
|---|---|
| **HISTORY** | Search for: ancient Arabia, Arab history, Sheba, Petra, country books on Yemen and Saudi Arabia (They usually have a chapter on the history of this period.)<br>☺ ☻ ☻ Thousand and One Arabian Nights edited by Andrew Lang. These tales were written down after the advent of Islam, but their origin is much older.<br>☻ King Solomon and the Queen of Sheba by Linda Tarry. Lots of legends and speculation surrounds these two powerful monarchs.<br>☻ The Road to Ubar: Finding the Atlantis of the Sands by Nicholas Clapp. A modern filmmaker becomes obsessed with finding an ancient city of Arabia which, according to legend, sunk into the sands when the city became so wicked that God destroyed it. The book touches on the ancient history and the modern condition of this part of the world.<br>☻ Literary History Of The Arabs by Reynold A. Nicholson. |
| **GEOGRAPHY** | Search for: rivers, lakes, specific rivers (Mississippi, Amazon, Lena, etc.), specific lakes (Great Lakes, Lake Baikal, Great Slave Lake, etc.), ponds, freshwater<br>☺ Rivers and Oceans: Geography Facts and Experiments by Barbara Taylor. Great simple projects to go along with your geography studies of rivers.<br>☺ Life in Ponds and Streams. A National Geographic book. This book follows Michael and his father as they search for life along a stream and pond in the woods. An oldie, but a goodie.<br>☺ ☻ Eye Wonder: Rivers and Lakes from DK Publishing. Great full color images and perfect snippets of information.<br>☻ Rivers and Lakes by David Cumming. Information from animals and plants to the uses people put to fresh water.<br>☺ The Mississippi: America's Mighty River by Robin Johnson. Look for other rivers in this geography series.<br>☻ Lakes and Rivers: A Freshwater Web of Life by Philip Johansson.<br>☺ Eyewitness Pond & River by Steve Parker. Awesome photography and just the right amount of detailed information for the middle grades.<br>☺ ☻ Rivers and Lakes by Neil Morris. |

| | |
|---|---|
| SCIENCE | Search for: atoms, molecules<br>☺ <u>What Are Atoms?</u> by Lisa Trumbauer.  Very short and very simple explanation of atoms.<br>☺ <u>What's Smaller Than a Pygmy Shrew?</u> by Robert E. Wells.  The author takes the reader through progressively smaller things until you end up with atoms and sub-atomic particles.<br>☺ <u>Molly and Wally Molecule</u> by Dean Badillo and Christine Adler.<br>☺ ● <u>How To Split the Atom</u> by Hazel Richardson.  Explanation of the history behind atomic discovery, how atoms are composed, and simple experiments to do at home.<br>☺ ● <u>Atomic Physics: Putting Together Atoms and Nuclei</u> by Professor Ima Kook.  A girl has a dream and when she wakes her mother explains the science behind the dream . . . an entertaining story containing complex scientific ideas.  Look for other books in this series by Professor Kook.<br>☺ ● <u>The Walt Disney Story of Our Friend the Atom</u> by Heinz Haber.  A nostalgic throwback to the 50's, the story is still relevant and entertaining to kids today.  Written for middle grades, but accessible to strong younger readers.<br>● <u>The Ever Changing Atom</u> by Roy A. Gallant.  An entertaining and clear explanation of atoms.<br>● <u>The Structure of Atoms</u> by Suzanne Slade.  Look for the companion chemistry books in this series as well.<br>● <u>God's Design For Chemistry: Properties of Atoms and Molecules</u> by Debbie Lawrence. If you're looking for something creation based, this is it.  This is the second in the chemistry series.  Look for the second edition if you want the experiments included.<br>● <u>Atom</u> by Isaac Asimov.  Out of print, look for a used copy or in your library. |
| THE ARTS | Search for: color, color theory<br>☺ <u>White Rabbit's Color Book</u> by Alan Baker.  Very basic color mixing in a story.<br>☺ <u>Mouse Paint</u> by Ellen Stole Walsh.  Three white mice find yellow, green, and blue paint and mix it up.<br>☺ ● <u>A Book About Color</u> by Mark Gonyea.  Covers mixing, value, complementary and more.<br>☺ ● <u>Using Color in Your Art</u> by Sandi Henry.  A hands-on project book using kids, adults, and great masters art to teach how to use color.<br>☺ ● <u>Color and How To Use It</u> by William F. Powell.  Simple and easy to understand, but thorough introduction to color theory for the beginner.<br>● <u>Color</u> by Betty Edwards.  Advanced methods for looking at color and explanation of how to use it properly in art.<br>● <u>An Eye For Color</u> by Olga Gutierrez De La Roza.  Uses actual art work and design pieces to teach color theory.<br>● <u>Color Choices: Making Color Sense Out of Color Theory</u> by Stephen Quiller. |

# HISTORY: ARABIANS

**Additional Layer**

When a particular language becomes the common language of business and diplomacy across many nations and cultures we say that language is the *lingua franca*.

*Lingua franca* originally meant language of the Franks, or Western Europeans and was first used during the Renaissance among the eastern Mediterranean.

Today English is considered the *lingua franca* of the world. For example, scientists, airplane pilots, and diplomats all learn English so they can communicate with one another.

In the ancient Middle East the *lingua franca* was Classical Arabic.

**Additional Layer**

The first recorded mention of the Arabian peoples that lived between Mesopotamia and Egypt is in the Book of Genesis in the Bible when Arabian merchants buy and sell Jacob's son, Joseph.

Arabia is perfectly positioned for trade between India, the Mediterranean, and Africa. The people there have taken advantage of their strategic placement for ages, growing rich since ancient times. Besides being traders, the Arabs were mostly nomadic tribes. They were shepherds of sheep, goats, and camels, and moved from place to place in search of water and grass. Though mostly nomadic, there were a few ancient Arab cities including Petra, the capital of Nabataea, and Ma'rib, the capital of Saba. At different times Arab tribes migrated longer distances and established more permanent nations, pushing out the original inhabitants in the process, as the Israelites and Canaanites of the Bible did (both Arabic Semitic tribes).

The kingdoms of Sheba (also called Saba and Sabaea), and Qataban in the south of the Arabian peninsula became wealthy through the cultivation of spice plants, myrrh, and frankincense, which were all very valuable and expensive. These southern kingdoms developed irrigation systems to keep the crops watered in a dry environment. These southern kingdoms were known as Arabia Felix (Happy Arabia) to the Romans.

Classical Arabic was spoken as the common language throughout the Middle East for many millennia, reaching back into ancient times. Jesus probably spoke Arabic most of the time. Today people all across the Muslim world are identified as Arabs by outsiders, but anciently only those tribes originating on the Arabian peninsula and the desert areas just north of there would have been considered Arabs, and even then only by others. They identified themselves as distinct tribes with similar cultures, but not politically allied or even related in most cases. Many Arabs do claim themselves to be descendents of Abraham however.

We think of Arabs today as synonymous with Muslims, but there were no ancient Muslims. (That religion was founded in the 7th century AD.) Anciently, Arabs worshiped a variety of gods from the one god of Abraham to the many gods of the Sumerians or other pagan gods.

☺ ☺ ☻ **EXPLORATION: Arabian Time Line**
Add a few dates to your time line:
- c. 1000 BC Arabs tame camels
- c. 500BC to 100AD Kingdom of Sheba reaches its height
- c. mid 900's BC Queen of Sheba, sometimes called Balqis, reigns

- c. 300BC to 100AD Incense Road flourishes
- c. 100BC to 150AD Kingdom of Nabataea becomes powerful.

## ☺ ☺ ☻ EXPLORATION: Ancient Arabian Map

Color a map of ancient Arabian nations and the Incense Road, an ancient Arabian trade route . Use the Ancient Arabia map from the end of this unit. Color the kingdoms of Sheba, Hadhramaut, Himyar, Aksum, Nabataea, and Qataban. Label the Rub' al Khali (Empty Quarter). Mark the trade routes taken for spices.

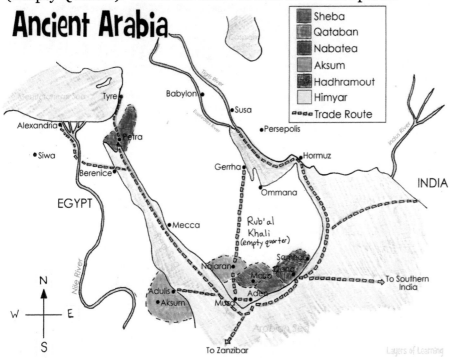

## ☺ ☺ ☻ EXPLORATION: Frankincense and Myrrh

Frankincense is a valuable spice produced from the resin of trees grown in the southern Arabian peninsula. At certain times of the year the trees are cut into and the sap oozes out of the cuts. The sap is then dried in the sun and ready to be used. Egyptians used the burnt spice to make kohl, which they placed around their eyes. The ancient Jews used the spice mixed with oil to represent eternal life and anointed new babies and the dead with it when they could afford it. These were desirable and widely used spices that were traded all over the known world at the time. This trade brought currency, art, and technology from all over into the Arabian region.

You can purchase frankincense and myrrh (or just take a trip and smell the bottles) from herbal stores so you can smell and see what the spices look like.

### Additional Layer

The traditional telling of the nativity story includes a moment where wise men from the East arrive and present the Christ child with gold, frankincense, and myrrh.

## Fabulous Fact

This seal ring was used by a Jew who lived in the city of Zaba, which is now in modern Yemen. The image is backward so that when pressed into wet wax or clay the image would come out facing correctly. It gives the name of the bearer and shows an image of a Jewish altar. The city of Zaba was a mixture of Jewish, Christian and Pagan faiths until the 7th century when Islam stormed through.

## Additional Layer

Dromedaries actually kneel down while passengers and cargo are being loaded on their backs. What service! Kneeling is about where the niceties stop though. They have a reputation for being stubborn and often spit, kick, run away, and stomp their feet. Learn about camels, first domesticated by the Arabs.

## ☺ ☻ EXPLORATION:  Arrival By Camel

Some of the earliest uses of camels as pack animals was in Arabia. They needed affordable ways of trading goods, and camels were the answer. Many of the lands they needed to travel through in order to trade were desert lands, and camels fared well through these dry regions.

Another name for the dromedary camel is the Arabian camel because it was domesticated on the Arabian Peninsula. Dromedaries (1 hump) can travel around 8 miles per hour while holding a rider. A Bactrian camel (2 humps) can travel only 2.5 miles per hour with a rider.

Pretend you are taking a trip by camel from Aden, Yemen to Alexandria, Egypt. If you could travel 10 hours per day, how many days would it take you on a dromedary? How many would it take you on a Bactrian camel? You can look up the mileage or use a map scale to determine the approximate distance.

## ☺ ☻ EXPLORATION: Arabia Felix

Arabia Felix or "Happy Arabia" was the nickname given to part of the Arabian peninsula, which is now modern day Yemen. This part is lusher and greener than the rest of the peninsula. It gets more rainfall than the rest. The people were also better at irrigating, and their fields were more productive than those of the regions around them. High sloping peaks, valleys, and riverbeds also help make the soil there more fertile.

On average, Arabia Felix gets around 40 inches of rain each year. Choose several locations around the globe, including the city you live in. Find out what the average rainfall is in these locations and chart them on a bar graph. Try to choose a variety of regions from across the globe: deserts, rainforests, plains, and mountainous areas.

## ☺ ☻ ☻ EXPLORATION: Glad To Get My Cinnamon In Aisle 12

Herodotus, an early historian, listed cinnamon as one of the products that came from the Arabians. He thought they got cinnamon from the nests of huge birds. The birds' nests were high on cliffs and nearly impossible to reach, so the Arabians cut up chunks of dead oxen and placed them below the nests. When the hungry birds flew down and brought the chunks back to their nests, the weight of the meat caused the nests to break apart and fall. Then the cinnamon from the nests could be gathered up from the ground.

I'm not sure where Herodotus got this idea, as cinnamon comes from either plants or tree bark, but it's a great story nonetheless. Cinnamon was important to the ancients as a medicine and in perfumes. Today herbalists still tout its health benefits, though we enjoy it more for its flavor.

Try this recipe for Cinnamon Snaps, a cookie that highlights the flavor of cinnamon.

<u>Ingredients:</u>
¾ cup shortening
1 cup packed brown sugar
1 egg
¼ cup molasses
2 ¼ cups flour
2 tsp. baking soda
2 tsp. cinnamon
½ tsp. salt
white sugar (optional)

1. In a large bowl, cream together the shortening and brown sugar, then beat in the egg and molasses.
2. Combine the flour, baking soda, cinnamon, and salt. Gradually add the dry ingredients into the creamed mixture.
3. Roll them into 1 inch balls. (If you want, you can roll the balls in sugar for a frosted look to the finished cookie.) Place them about 2 inches apart on an ungreased baking sheet. Bake at 350 degrees for about 10 minutes. The tops will crack a little when they're done.

Now give cinnamon snaps a taste!

### ☺ ☻ EXPLORATION: Petra

Petra is an intriguing city, carved within rocks and cliffs in the middle of the desert. The word Petra means "rock." How fitting. It was founded by the Nabataeans who turned the city into a bustling trading center. It was located right along prominent trade routes. Anciently the Nabataeans also built a system of

**Fabulous Fact**
Before Islam, the people in the far south spoke four distinct languages. Today the languages are extinct, having been replaced by Classical Arabic with the coming of Islam.

**Famous Folks**
Read about Balqis, the Queen of Sheba. She is spoken of in the Bible, the Qur'an and by the people of Ethiopia. They all have different tales and views of this famous woman, but there is no doubt she was powerful and influential.

*Fresco of the Queen of Sheba traveling to visit Solomon, from a wall in Ethiopia.*

**Writer's Workshop**

Create your own idea of how resourceful Arabians could have gotten the cinnamon down had it really been in giant birds' nest.

Write about it in your writer's notebook.

## Additional Layer

Handel wrote a musical piece entitled "Arrival of the Queen of Sheba".

You can listen to it here:http://youtu.be/-TGKJ9MgCOQ

## Additional Layer

Though the religions of the Arabs were varied and often borrowed from others, there was a purely Arabic mythology as well.

The chief god was Allah, later considered the only god by Islam; during earlier times he was the creator god and the bringer of rain.

Allat was the goddess of Mecca and daughter of Allah.

Al'Uzza was the fertility goddess.

Manat was the goddess of fate and Arab children were often named after her to bring good luck.

Jinn were powerful spirit beings living in a world parallel to humans and along with angels and humans were creatures made by Allah.

Nasnas, ghouls, and bahamut are three types of monsters or demons which are always antagonistic toward humans.

dams and cisterns to hold the water that rained down in flash floods in the area. They then sold the water during droughts, making the city a prosperous one.

The entrance to the city is through a narrow gorge flanked by tall cliffs. The buildings are mostly cut right out of the rock. The larger ones survived the centuries, though the houses have mostly been destroyed by earthquakes over time. Between the earthquakes that destroyed their homes and water systems, and alternate oversea trade routes coming into existence, the city was eventually forgotten. In 1812 it was rediscovered and is now a tourist site that gives people a taste of ancient life.

Closer examination of the rocks at Petra reveal that they are sedimentary, sandstone to be exact. How can you tell it's sedimentary? Look at the above picture. It's very easy to see the many layers of rock. These were formed by the wind moving the sand, mixing with minerals, and being exposed to heat and pressure. You can also see many colors in the stone from the variety of plants and animals that died and were buried within the rock sediments.

Get a quart size, wide mouth, glass mason jar and fill it with uncooked rice about ¾ of the way full. Now push a rubber bouncy ball deep into the rice so it's buried. Put the jar on the table and shake it back and forth. What happens? Why?

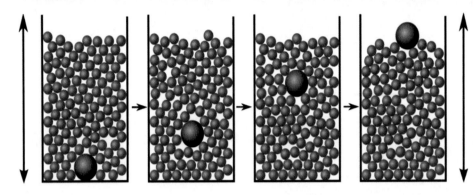

This phenomenon is called the Brazil Nut Effect. When you open a can of mixed nuts, the Brazil nuts (the largest) are always on top of the can. The smaller nuts settle down lower. This is also true of sedimentary rock like that found at Petra. The lower layers are made of the smallest rock – sand. The sand has been pressed together to form sandstone. The upper layers are made of increasingly larger bits of rock.

## ☺ ☻ EXPLORATION: Petra Poetry

John William Burgon's poem, *Petra,* describes the city quite accurately right down to the rose-colored hue of the rocks it's carved out of. Believe it or not, he had never seen it when he wrote the poem.

> It seems no work of Man's creative hand,
> by labour wrought as wavering fancy planned;
> But from the rock as if by magic grown,
> eternal, silent, beautiful, alone!
> Not virgin-white like that old Doric shrine,
> where erst Athena held her rites divine;
> Not saintly-grey, like many a minster fane,
> that crowns the hill and consecrates the plain;
> But rose-red as if the blush of dawn,
> that first beheld them were not yet withdrawn;
> The hues of youth upon a brow of woe,
> which Man deemed old two thousand years ago,
> match me such marvel save in Eastern clime,
> a rose-red city half as old as time.

Look at some pictures of Petra and brain storm descriptive words about the city using the five senses. Then use these words to fill in the blanks to make a poem about Petra. (adjust the poem as needed for your description.)

> It seems to be a city of _____ .
>
> Looking as though made by _____ .

## Additional Layer

Arab tradition has it that Petra was the place where Moses used his staff to strike a rock, causing water to come out for the thirsty Hebrews.

*Moses Striking the Rock*
by Pieter de Grebber
(1630)

## Additional Layer

Part of *Indiana Jones and The Last Crusade* was filmed in Petra in 1989.

## Additional Layer

Arabia is very dry, some areas so dry that they are empty of people and have very few plants or animals. Learn more about deserts.

## Fabulous Fact

The Byzantines, Sassanids, and Persians were routinely fighting each other and all three used Bedouin Arabs as allies. The Byzantines preferred tribes of Christians, though in the end, the differences in their brands of Christianity divided them and this division contributed to the weakening of the Byzantine Empire just as Islam was on the rise.

*Rub al Khalid, the Empty Quarter. Photo by Javierblas and shared under cc license.*

## Fabulous Fact

A Bedouin tent was woven from goats hair, which contracts and becomes water proof when it gets wet. It also is a great insulator, keeping the heat out in the day and the heat from the fire in at night.

*Photo by Etan J. Tal and shared under cc license.*

I smell the _____ of the desert.

I feel the _____ in the stones.

I can taste the _____ in the air.

### ☺ ☺ ☻ EXPEDITION: Touring Petra

If you ever have the chance, put Petra on your list of places to see before you die. It is one of the most intriguing cities in the world with its rich history and interesting geography. If a trip to Petra isn't in the cards today, you can go take a virtual tour at the American Museum of Natural History's website. Go to http://www.amnh.org/exhibitions/past-exhibitions/petra.

### ☺ ☻ EXPLORATION: Bedouins

The Bedouin people of central Arabia were nomads. There was not enough rain to settle into one place and so they herded their flocks from well to oasis, from mountain to desert, depending on the season. These people followed different religions ranging from Judaism to Christianity to the pagan beliefs handed down from the Sumerians. Their lineage was always traced through the female line. They spoke Arabic and were Semitic in race, like the Hebrew Kingdoms. Outsiders often lumped them together as one race, but they would have seen each tribe as a completely separate political entity based roughly on family relationships.

Build a Bedouin tent from blankets in your living room, put on a Bedouin headdress and read a story from the Arabian Nights together. You'll also find a Bedouin traveler coloring sheet in the printables at the end of the unit.

# GEOGRAPHY: RIVERS & LAKES

Rivers and lakes are important both to wildlife and people. They are used for fresh water to drink and irrigate plants, and also in commerce and energy production. Unfortunately, people have sometimes used these resources unwisely as dumping grounds for chemicals and sewage as well. By and large people are learning from these mistakes and taking better care of resources than ever before.

*This is the Limpopo River in Africa.*

In this unit we'll learn where some lakes and rivers are located, about the land form types associated with fresh water, and about how people use fresh water sources.

### ☺ ☺ ☻ EXPLORATION: Mapping the Rivers
At the end of this unit is a map of the rivers of the world. On the map the largest rivers on each continent are listed. Kids should use a student atlas to determine where each river is located and then label the rivers.

### ☺ ☺ ☻ EXPLORATION: My Rivers
Get a blank map of your state or region (you can find outline maps of the states, provinces, and many countries at www.Layers-of-Learning.com). Using a student atlas, draw in and label the major rivers in your area.

Which river is nearest to you? Where does it flow from? Where does it empty into? Does it have any tributaries? Looking at a map of your area, can you trace the drainage basin?

## Additional Layer

Human impact on natural lakes and rivers can be dramatic. The Aral Sea used to be one of the largest lakes in the world. But in the 1960's the Soviets diverted many of the rivers that fed the sea for irrigation projects. Today the Aral Sea has nearly dried up.

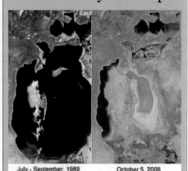

July - September, 1989      October 5, 2008

*Images by NASA*

The picture on the left shows the Aral Sea in 1989. The picture on the right shows the Aral Sea in 2008.

There are now projects underway to save the sea. Learn more about the actual impact the loss of this large lake has had on wildlife and on humans.

## Fabulous Fact

Fish that live part of their life in freshwater and part in sea water are called androgynous.

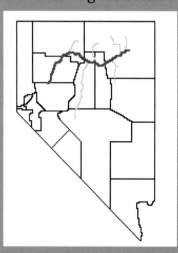
☻ ☻ ☻ **EXPLORATION: A Bend in the River**

Below we've defined many land features associated with fresh water. Putting one definition on each page, create a booklet or pamphlet describing each of these features. Illustrate it with appropriate pictures.

*The Colorado River in the United States travels through a deep canyon.*

Canyon: a steep sided gully, eroded by running water. Usually there is an active river at the bottom of a canyon.

Delta: a fan shaped formation where a river flows into the sea. The river splits into many different streams, leaving sediment behind and forming islands.

Ford: a shallow place where a river may be crossed on foot.

Headwater: also called a source, it is the place where a stream begins, usually with a spring or with glacier run-off.

Lake: a large inland body of fresh water. Small lakes are called ponds and even smaller bodies of water are called pools.

Marsh: an area of very wet ground, low lying and level, covered with thick grasses and water plants interspersed with pools and puddles of water.

Meander: a bend in a winding course of a slow moving river. Meanders occur when a river flows through a plain as opposed to through mountainous country. Sometimes a meander will be cut off from the main river by erosion creating an oxbow lake.

Mouth: where a river empties out into a lake, the ocean or

another river.

Rapids: a section of a river with swift rough flowing water over rocks.

Stream: any body of swiftly flowing water. A river is a large stream; brooks and creeks are small streams.

Watershed: All the land drained of water by a particular system of rivers which flow together and ultimately to the sea.

Waterfall: a portion of a stream that flows over the edge of a cliff or a series of smaller drop offs. A cataract is a large dramatic waterfall. A cascade is a series of smaller waterfalls.

### ☺ ☺ ☺ EXPLORATION: Been There!
Make a list of all the rivers and lakes you have visited on trips. Find each of these places on a map. As you study them look along the river and see if you can find place names that end in "River" or "Mouth" or "Falls" or any other river words.

### ☺ ☺ ☺ EXPEDITION: Go Jump In A Lake
Visit a river or lake near you. Find a state, Corp of Engineers, or NPS park nearby. What should you do when you're there? Well, bring a picnic, a fishing pole, a bucket, a net for catching things, and your curiosity. Just explore and have fun. Sometimes the best way to fall in love with a place is just to enjoy it, not cram for it.

But say you do want to pack a bit more education in . . .

*   Bring guide books for identifying plants, insects, birds, etc.
*   Search the banks or shore for animal tracks
*   In the spring look for tadpoles
*   Beforehand learn what the lake/river is used for. Logging? Fishing? Recreation? Irrigation? Transport? Drinking water?
*   Find out about the history of the place. Who first settled the area? What industries were there? When was the park you visited built?
*   Learn about about the ecology of the site. Is pollution a problem or was it in the past? Are there any endangered or rare animals or plants in the area? Are there problems with invasive plant or animal species?
*   Take a sample of the water home with you and pop it under a microscope. Make a diagram showing what you

**Additional Layer**
If you're going to be near the water it would be a good idea to remind kids about water safety. Even people who are great swimmers can drown if they aren't careful.

1. Have a buddy with you.

2. If you are in a boat, wear a life jacket. In most states by law you don't have to wear a life jacket if you are an adult, but it's one of those things—does the government really have to tell you not to be careless?

3. Know what's in the water before you go in. Is it shallow or deep? Are there undercurrents, sharp objects, or pollution?

4. Stay Dry: Actually, you can get wet, just be sure you have a way to get dry and warm again to avoid hypothermia.

Here are some rivers in art:

*The Banks of the Oise (c. 1877) Alfred Sisley*

*View of Trento (1494) Albrect Dürer*

*Indian At Sunset (1847) Thomas Cole*

*Winter Landscape From Bystra (1910) Julian Falat*

Paint your own river picture.

observed under the microscope.

• Take along a sketchbook on your outing and spend some time in observation and sketching what you see. You could even bring paints and make a watercolor painting of what you observe.

☺ ☻ **EXPERIMENT: Rivers Change**

The boundaries and beds of rivers change over time. When water flows it erodes land from upstream, carries it downstream, and deposits it lower down.

You can show this process.

You need:
• soil and small rocks mixed together
• a long container (an underbed storage box for wrapping paper is ideal) or a sloping hill outside
• water

Place your soil and rocks into the container, dampen it and press it together to make it firm. Give the box a gentle slope. Pour water from a gallon jug or pitcher onto the upper end of the slope and watch as the water runs down in streams. Observe how the land is eroded, how sediment is carried down stream, and how it is deposited lower down.

What happens if the slope is steeper? Shallower? What if the land is heavily planted with thick grass vs. bare soil?

### River Stages: Erosion, Transport, Deposition

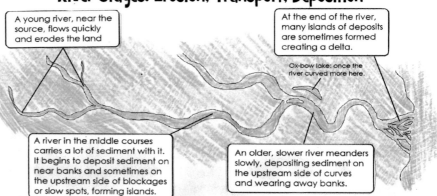

A young river, near the source, flows quickly and erodes the land

At the end of the river, many islands of deposits are sometimes formed creating a delta.

Ox-bow lake: once the river curved more here.

A river in the middle courses carries a lot of sediment with it. It begins to deposit sediment on near banks and sometimes on the upstream side of blockages or slow spots, forming islands.

An older, slower river meanders slowly, depositing sediment on the upstream side of curves and wearing away banks.

Have the kids color the River Stages diagram showing the three stages of river building and point out the meanders and ox bow lakes. The descriptions of the river stages are out of order. Kids need to read them, cut them out and glue them back on in the correct order.

If you live near a river you can collect water from the river in a clear container with a lid. Allow the river water to sit still for a day. The sediment should settle to the bottom. It would be interesting to repeat this experiment at different seasons of the year. Is there more sediment at some times than at others? Is there more sediment or less in a lake on the same river system?

### ☺ ◉ EXPLORATION: Fishin' for Answers

Play a fishing game as a review or in place of a test after you have read a few books on rivers and lakes and done an activity or two. First you need to print out the fish cards you'll find at the end of this unit. One sheet of fish has questions about rivers and lakes already printed on it. You can cut out more simple fish shapes if you want to create more of your own questions. Cut out the fish and glue them onto stiffer paper, like colored card stock. (If you'd like, you can color code them according to difficulty, with tougher questions being worth more points.) Attach a paper clip to each fish.

Now you need a fishing pole. Tie a string to one end of a short stick and hot glue the string to a small magnet, like a button magnet.

Place the fish upside down, so the questions are concealed, into a "pond". You can use a small empty kiddie pool as a pond or a blue blanket spread on the floor. Have the kids take turns fishing for questions. If the player gets the answer right she keeps the fish. If she misses it, read the answer, throw the fish back, and try again.

### ☺ EXPLORATION: Otter Antics

Read a book about animals that live in rivers and lakes. Then play river animal charades. Each child takes a turn being a river animal. Everyone else tries to guess who they are.

**Fabulous Facts**

The longest river in the world is the Nile. The longest river in the U.S. is the Missouri.

Arguably the three most polluted rivers on earth are the Yangtze in China and the Ganges and Indus rivers in India.

If you count the lakes along it, the Lawrence river system holds more water than any other on earth.

Navigable rivers like the Mississippi often have to be dredged as they fill up with so much sediment carried downstream and deposited as the river slows.

*Where the Mississippi and the Ohio meet, NASA.*

**Additional Layer**

If you live in the Middle East, most of the rivers you know about are ephemeral, or only appear during rainy seasons. Permanent rivers are called "rivers of water" to distinguish them from dry river beds.

## Additional Layer

The use of dams in rivers is very controversial. Many people are worried about how dams affect the ecology of a river. Others are worried about the cost of building dams. Still others are worried about how the dam will affect water usage for humans, including commerce, recreation, and irrigation. In the end, the building, maintenance, and usage of dams is always political. If there is a dam near you, find out when it was built and whether there was any controversy over it. Find out if there is any controversy over it now. What do you think about dams on rivers? Remember to weigh all sides of the argument.

## On the Web

Go to http://renewourrivers.com/wp-content/uploads/2010/05/ROR-Color-Book-Teachers-Lesson-Plan.pdf for a printable coloring book and lesson plan about pollution that was inspired by an message found in a bottle. The bottle spurred the beginning of many river clean-up projects.

## ☺ ☻ EXPLORATION: River Animals

Select a river animal and learn about its habitat. Here are some you may consider: wood duck, salmon, great blue heron, midland water snake, bullfrog, snapping turtle, red-eared slider, southern two-lined salamander, longnose gar, striped shiner, channel catfish, largemouth bass, smallmouth bass, rainbow darter, water strider, water boatman, threeridge mussel, snail, crayfish, mink, beaver. Learn about the habitat of your animal and find out specific needs that are met by the river and its characteristics, including the bottom composition, temperature of the water, clarity, the depth and speed of the river, and the surrounding land and vegetation. How does the habitat supports the animal's basic needs of air, food, water, shelter, and reproduction? Design a model that showcases the habitat and how it meets the animal's needs. You can use natural materials, clay, paint, or anything else you wish inside a sturdy box.

## ☺ ☻ ☻ EXPEDITION: Dams

Visit a dam near you. Most dams do tours. Read a book or two on dams before hand so you know enough to ask good questions.

We recently went on a tour of Albeni Falls Dam near Priest River, Idaho. We found out that the concrete deep inside the dam still hasn't dried, more than 50 years later! We also found out that the power generated at this dam near our house actually gets sent hundreds and hundreds of miles away to big cities. We don't get any of it. And finally, we found out that in this post 9-11 world you can't be told how many people work at the dam or when the shifts begin and end or who any of the employees are.

We've also visited Boundary Dam and Grand Coulee Dam in the past and each trip was absolutely fascinating.

## ☺ ☻ ☻ EXPLORATION: People Use Lakes and Rivers

Since ancient times we've relied on rivers and lakes to provide us with water for drinking, cleaning, transportation, and irrigation. Sometimes they were also used for protection; because it wasn't easy to cross, enemies could be kept away. Civilizations and cities have often sprung up near bodies of water for these reasons.

We use rivers and lakes for many things. Just like the ancients, we drink, clean, transport, and irrigate from them. We also use them for recreation – fishing, swimming, boating, kayaking, rafting, and more. We use them to provide us with hydroelectric power. They are in many ways, a life source for us.

Choose a river or lake in your area. Find out how it is used and some of its history.  Write a pamphlet about all that you find out.

### ☺ ☺ ☻ EXPLORATION: River Legends

There are many legends and stories about rivers.  One, called
*How the Fly Saved the River*, goes like this:

*Many years ago when the world was still quite new, there was a
beautiful river. Fish filled this river, and its water was so pure
and sweet that all the animals came there to drink.
A giant moose heard about the river and he couldn't resist
coming for a drink of the sweet water. But he was so big, and he
drank so much, that soon the water began to sink lower and
lower - down and down it went.*

*The beavers were worried. With the water disappearing, soon
their lodges would be destroyed.*

*The muskrats were worried. What would they do if the water
vanished? How could they live?*

*The fish were worried. The other animals could live on land if
the water dried up, but they couldn't.*

*How could they drive the giant moose from the river?  He was
so big that they were too afraid to try. Even the bear trembled at
the thought.*

*At last the fly determined to drive the moose away.  The animals
laughed and jeered.  How could a tiny fly frighten a giant
moose?  The fly said nothing, but that day he went into action.*

*He landed on the moose's foreleg and bit sharply.  The moose
stamped his foot harder, and each time he stamped, the ground
sank and the water rushed in to fill it up. Then the fly jumped
about all over the moose, biting and biting and biting until the
moose could stand no more. He dashed madly about the banks
of the river, shaking his head, stamping his feet, snorting and
blowing. At last the moose fled from the river, and never did
come back.*

*The fly was very proud and boasted to the other animals, "Even
the small can fight the strong if they use their brains to think."*

Write and illustrate your own river legend.

### On the Web

The BBC has a simple
printable worksheet
where kids can define
deposition,
transportation, and
erosion.

http://www.bbc.co.uk/sc
hools/riversandcoasts/w
orksheets/change_river.s
html

### Fabulous Fact

Lake Superior is the
largest freshwater lake in
the world, but
surprisingly, there is
another lake that holds
even more freshwater
than Superior.

*Lake Superior, USA*

Lake Baikal is a large
lake in Asia that holds
the most freshwater in
the world.  It is the
deepest lake in the world,
and because of its depth,
it holds more water.

*Lake Baikal, Russia*

# SCIENCE: ATOMS

## Fabulous Fact
People have been looking for the fundamental building blocks of matter since ancient times. Fundamental means the most basic, simple; there are no smaller parts. Generally people want the fundamental to be simple and elegant, not complicated and messy.

## On The Web
http://www.nclark.net/Atom
This site has a ton of great activities and excellent worksheets about atomic structure.

## Famous Folks
John Dalton was one of the earliest scientists to form a hypothesis regarding atoms and their properties. He was mostly right and partly wrong.

Atoms are the smallest units that give characteristics to the stuff they make up. Atoms are, in turn, made up of smaller particles: protons and neutrons in the center (called the nucleus) and electrons that whiz around in a cloud around the nucleus. The protons, neutrons, and electrons are made up of even smaller parts.

Electrons are arranged around the nucleus in various levels of energy. The first level can hold up to two electrons, each level after that can hold up to eight electrons. The electron level, or shell, as chemists call it, wants to be full. An atom with a less than full electron shell will steal or share in order to be stable. We call this stealing (or sharing) bonding.

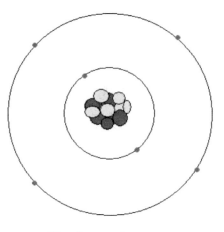

### Carbon Atom
6 protons, 6 neutrons, 6 electrons

When atoms are combined with other atoms, that makes molecules; and molecules joined together makes the stuff we can see, touch, or feel.

## ☺ ☺ ☻ EXPLORATION:  The Structure of Stuff
To demonstrate what atomic structure is like, get a bunch of grapes with seeds. The atom is like the grape. Atoms are made of parts. These parts are electrons, neutrons, and protons. These are called sub-atomic particles because they are smaller than an

atom. There are even smaller parts, but that would lead us into quarks, string theory, and super string theory and we won't go there.

Back to the grape. The seeds inside are like the neutrons and protons. Neutrons are neutral, they have no charge. Protons are positively charged. Electrons are negatively charged. The electrons zoom around in a cloud around the neutrons and protons, together called the nucleus. The flesh of the grape is like the electron cloud.

The opposite charges of the protons and electrons is one of the forces holding the atom together. There are other forces called the strong and weak force, but again, that's more in depth than we'll go for now.

### ☻ EXPLORATION: More Atomic Structure

The electrons in an atom can mathematically be literally anywhere in space, but there are certain areas where they have a high probability of existing. We call these areas "shells". There is a worksheet at the end of this unit that shows what the shells in an atom look like. The lowest energy shells, those closest to the nucleus are S shells. Next are P shells and then D shells and finally F shells, which are so complex that we didn't put them on the worksheet. Inside each shell up to two electrons can exist.

Learn more about shells by watching this series from Khan Academy:https://www.khanacademy.org/science/chemistry/orbi tals-and-electrons. We also really like the *A Self-Teaching Guide: Chemistry* book by Clifford C. Houk and Richard Post. The relevant chapter is Chapter 1.

After you watch or read, color the energy shells printable and complete the "Filling the Electron Shells" worksheet, both from the end of this unit.

Answers to the "Electron Shells" worksheet are also in the printables at the end of this unit.

### ☺ ☻ EXPERIMENT: Opposites Attract

To demonstrate electric charges and their attractive and repellent quality, get a comb, some paper, and a hole punch.

1. Punch some holes out of the paper and spread them out on the table or counter top.
2. Run a comb through your hair several times.
3. Bring the comb close to the paper dots and watch them jump off the counter and cling to the comb.

The comb picks up electrons from your hair, making the comb negatively charged. Remember, adding electrons will give something a negative charge because electrons carry negative charges. The same thing happens when you run a balloon over your hair. The paper dots carry a positive charge. The negative charges from those electrons attract the positive charges of the paper, making them attracted to each other.

## Explanation

For birthdays and Christmas we often give our kids educational gifts. No way are they boring.

Consider Snap Circuits, Legos, Erector sets, dinosaur fossil excavation kits, chemistry kits, binoculars, how-to-draw books, a rock hammer and rock identification guide, books, and a bird feeder.

Science and art gifts are especially fun, but dress-up costumes, puppets, building toys, and magazine subscriptions are cool too. Think about your kids' interests and use the money you'd usually spend on Barbie or Transformers to buy something a little more lasting, something that will really feed their curiosity.

*Scientifics* and *Home Science Tools* are our favorite science suppliers.

And check out your local craft and hobby shops for more.

*Michelle*

## Fabulous Fact

The Greek root for the word atom is atomon, which means "cannot be divided". Of course we now know that atoms can be divided, but it was too late, the name stuck.

However, chemically, an atom cannot be divided. That is, there is no chemical reaction that will split an atom. For atom splitting we turn to physics.

## Famous Folks

Ernest Rutherford was the discoverer of the atom's nucleus and its positive charge.

Rutherford was born and raised in New Zealand, to poor parents who insisted on great education for their children. Rutherford spent his adult life in Britain where laboratories and scientific societies and universities existed that could fund his work.

## ☺ ☻ EXPLORATION: Atomic Mobile

Choose an element and make a mobile out of its electrons, protons, and neutrons. You'll want to stick with the simpler elements, the ones that have a lower atomic number.

Hydrogen: 1 proton, 1 electron
Lithium: 3 neutrons, 3 protons, 3 electrons
Carbon: 4 neutrons, 4 protons, 4 electrons
Oxygen: 8 neutrons, 8 protons, 8 electrons
Neon: 10 neutrons, 10 protons, 10 electrons

Use small foam balls from the craft store for your atom's parts. The electrons should be less than half the size of the parts in the nucleus (they're actually MUCH smaller in proportion to the nucleus, but half will have to do.)

### Lithium (Li)

paper plate

The first two electrons are closer to the neucleus, in the lowest energy level.

These represent the protons (red) and the neutrons (yellow).

Paint all your neutrons in one color, all your protons in another color, and all your electrons in a third color.

Suspend your nucleus parts in the center of the mobile from a paper plate held horizontally. Suspend the first two electrons near the nucleus, but not touching. And suspend up to the next eight in a ring outside the first two electrons.

## ☺ ☻ EXPLORATION: Timeline of Atomic Discovery

On a long sheet of paper (freezer paper or something similar) draw a line from one side to the other midway down the paper. Label the line in increments from 1800 to 1950. Place each of these atomic discovery events on your timeline. Cut out, color, and glue on the timeline images of the atom from the end of this unit to show the conceptual development of the atom.

- 1803 John Dalton proposes the concept of spherical atoms with unique properties that make up the building blocks of everything else.
- 1869 Dmitri Mendeleev developed the idea that atoms can be arranged in periods (as in the periodic table) according to their weights and properties.
- 1894 G.J. Stoney discovered flowing negative particles he

named electrons.

- 1911 Ernest Rutherford discovered the nucleus of the atom and assumed the electrons were located outside the nucleus.
- 1914 H.G.J. Mosely discovered that the number of protons in the nucleus is equal to the atomic number of an atom.
- 1922 Neils Bohr discovers that electrons are arranged in levels, or shells, around the nucleus.
- 1930 Schrodinger developed the concept of an electron cloud as opposed to specific points where an electron might be found.
- 1932 James Chadwick discovered the neutron.
- Further developments regarding strong and weak forces, quarks and strings, and so on have taken place after 1950. Have your high schooler research when these developments happened.

## ☺ ☻ EXPLORATION: Isotopes

Every element has a specific number of protons, neutrons and electrons. But sometimes the number of neutrons changes. These variations are called isotopes. The neutrons don't affect the properties of the element, so an isotope of carbon is still carbon. Nearly every element has isotopes that occur naturally. Some of them are stable and others are radioactive.

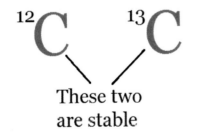

These two are stable

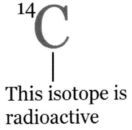

This isotope is radioactive

Carbon atoms occur naturally in three forms. Carbon-12 is the most common form of carbon, with 6 neutrons. Carbon-13 and Carbon-14 are isotopes with 7 neutrons and 8 neutrons, respectively. Carbon-14 is radioactive, which means it gives off neutrons until it reaches a stable form. Carbon isotopes in many other variations have been formed in labs as well.

$$6 \quad C \quad \begin{matrix} 2 \\ 4 \end{matrix}$$

12.0107

The atomic number, below the symbol for carbon, C, on the periodic table is 12.0107. That means the average

---

**Fabulous Fact**

If you drew an atom to scale and made the nucleus 1 cm across. The electron cloud would be larger than a football field. Most of the space in an atom is just space, not stuff.

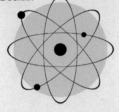

**Fabulous Fact**

Physicists are coming across new particles all the time. We have photons and prions, muons and neutrinos and a couple dozen more specific types of particles. There are so many that most of them are just given a Greek letter to specify them.

**On The Web**

Go to You Tube to see a plethora of videos on Ernest Rutherford's Gold Foil Experiment that led to the discovery of the nucleus of an atom.

Here's our favorite video on this subject:

http://www.youtube.com/watch?NR=1&v=zn0xGIxoZSo

There are fancier videos, but this one explains all the important information perfectly.

## Deep Thoughts

What are the smallest, most fundamental pieces of matter? We're still not sure.

We do know that protons and neutrons are made of smaller pieces of matter, which are named quarks. Scientists are pretty sure quarks are the smallest. There are six types of quarks, named down, up, strange, charm, bottom, and top. Electrons are also thought to be fundamental. The truth is though that we can't be sure. Maybe someone will find something smaller in the future.

*Model of a neutron showing the quarks that compose it.*

## Turning Lead Into Gold?

Alchemists of the middle ages and earlier believed in transmutation, which is the changing of one element into another.

Mostly this is nonsense. However, there are a proportionally small number of atoms of each element that are radioactive and decay so violently that they do actually transmutate, changing the number of protons in a nucleus.

weight of carbon atoms in the natural world is just a little above the most common weight of 12. The weight of 12 is based on 6 protons and 6 neutrons. It's the presence of a few isotopes of Carbon 13 and Carbon 14 that bring the average up.

Prepare some "atoms" ahead of time, by putting two different colored pompoms into zip-close sandwich bags. The bags represent the nucleus of the atom. In the example below, the yellow pompoms represent protons and the orange represent neutrons. Tell the student what each color you choose represents. Then ask them to identify which element they were given and which isotope of that element they have. To find the answer they have to count the number of protons to find the element, then the total number of protons and neutrons together to find the isotope.

Here are some isotopes to consider:

| Atom | Protons | Neutrons |
| --- | --- | --- |
| Carbon-12 | 6 | 6 |
| Carbon-13 | 6 | 7 |
| Carbon-14 | 6 | 8 |
| Helium-3 | 2 | 1 |
| Helium-4 | 2 | 2 |
| Oxygen -16 | 8 | 8 |
| Oxygen-17 | 8 | 9 |
| Oxygen-18 | 8 | 10 |
| Beryllium-8 | 4 | 4 |
| Beryllium-9 | 4 | 5 |
| Nitrogen-14 | 7 | 7 |
| Nitrogen-15 | 7 | 8 |

After the students have identified several isotopes, have them create their own pompom isotopes. They can look up naturally occurring isotopes on the internet.

## ☺ ☺ ☻ EXPLORATION: Marshmallow Molecules

For a basic lesson on molecules, all you need are some colored mini marshmallows and toothpicks. This simple, hands-on activity will show how atoms combine to form molecules, and also help students understand how simple chemical formulas are written. First, explain that when atoms join together (or bond) they make up molecules. Assign a different color of marshmallow for different elements.

Pink=Nitrogen

Yellow=Carbon

Orange=Oxygen

Green=Hydrogen

If you make up a little chart showing these designations it will simplify things for the kids (it doesn't really matter which colors you assign for the elements). Using 2 green marshmallows (hydrogens) and 1 orange marshmallow (oxygen), show them what a water bond looks like.

The toothpicks are used to poke into the marshmallows and hold them together. Now have them write the chemical formula ($H_2O$), which simply means that 2 hydrogens and 1 oxygen have joined together to make 1 molecule of water. The number that <u>follows</u> the atomic letter designates how many of that kind of atom there are.

### Explanation

Robert Boyle wrote in the *Skeptical Chemyst* that he rejected the ancient idea of earth, air, water and fire and the basic elements that make up all matter.

Boyle was a first generation chemist, taking over from the more mystical alchemist tradition of earlier ages.

When criticized for withholding strong opinions he said this:

*But I blush not to acknowledge that I much lesse scruple to confess that I Doubt, when I do so, then to profess that I Know what I do not: And I should have much stronger Expectations then I dare yet entertain, to see Philosophy solidly establish't, if men would more carefully distinguish those things that they know, from those that they ignore or do but think, and then explicate clearly the things they conceive they understand, acknowledge ingenuously what it is they ignore, and profess so candidly their Doubts, that the industry of intelligent persons might be set on work to make further enquiries, and the easiness of less discerning Men might not be impos'd on.*

Boyle didn't think scientists or philosophers should pretend to know for certain things that they only guess at. We agree.

**Definition**
Strictly speaking, "molecule" refers only to covalently bonded atoms, but we're going to ignore that in these units and refer to all bonded atoms as molecules.

**Additional Layer**
Most molecules are microscopic, but a few can reach larger sizes, large enough to be seen with the naked eye. DNA is one of these macromolecules. We'll isolate and look at DNA in Year 2 when we study the human body.

**Additional Layer**
• Molecules always exist in ratios of whole numbers. For example, water always exists in ratios of two hydrogen molecules to one oxygen molecule.

**On the Web**
This video on atomic structure is excellent for middle grades and up. http://youtu.be/h6LPAw AmnCQ
And this video from the same guy explains the difference between an atom and a molecule:http://youtu.be /RbbOBPfH_uk

**On the Web**
For younger kids: http://youtu.be/vlSOES XQI7o

Give them the chemical formulas for several other common molecules to try on their own.

This is carbon dioxide, which you breath out. It ahs double bonds which means the atoms are sharing two sets of electrons and not just one.

*these bonds are
actually double bonds*

This is ammonia, which you probably use to clean your glass.

This is sugar, which is a long chain of carbon surrounded by hydrogen and oxygen.

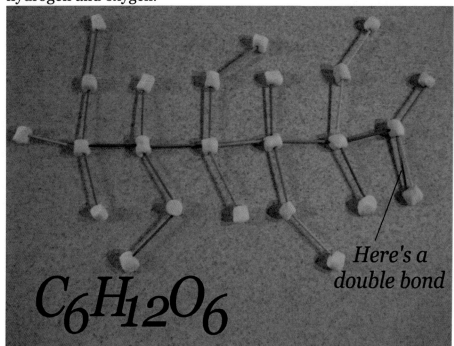

$C_6H_{12}O_6$

*Here's a double bond*

Each time they make the molecule have them write its chemical formula as well. At this point it's okay if they're made-up molecules. The point is to understand how atoms combine into molecules.

When they've made each of the example molecules, let them make their own molecules! Kids will love coming up with their own long and crazy chemical formulas and then trying to piece them together according to their formula.

Point out to the kids that each Hydrogen has one bond, each carbon has four bonds, each oxygen has two bonds and each nitrogen has three bonds.

*Unit 1.14 goes into more depth on the bonding process, for now just concentrate on the concept that atoms combine to make molecules.*

☺ ☻ **EXPERIMENT: Make a Molecule From Atoms**
You can combine atoms of the elements iron (Fe) and Sulfur (S) into molecules. For this experiment you need:

- sulfur and iron filings, both of which you can get from a science supplier like Carolina Biological Supply or Home Science Tools.

### Explanation

Molecules are three dimensional and always have the same bond lengths and bond angles for a particular molecule.

The marshmallow molecules and other molecule images in this unit do not reflect what a molecule actually looks like. These are just representations of a molecule.

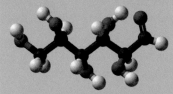

The above 3-dimensional representation is closer to how an actual sugar molecule would look. At least it is the right shape, but the colors and the little ball representing the atoms and the sticks representing the bonds are not true to life.

### Additional Layer

Sugar is the most easily absorbed form of energy for the human body. It also has nothing else in it except for energy; no vitamins or minerals. When our bodies have gleaned the current required energy, the rest is stored as fat. Scientists think that sugar is the only food we are born craving.

## Explanation

Laboratory equipment is not always necessary for experiments in science, but be careful, sometimes it is.

Experiments whether in this book or others, will tell you which materials to use. Some experiments require precise measurements and graduated cylinders or electronic scales are necessary. Some experiments require heat and normal glass or plastic bowls will not stand up and metal vessels may react with your experiment having unintended and perhaps dangerous results.

Other experiments require special apparatus, simply not available at the grocery store.

## Fabulous Fact

The iron in cereal is usually elemental iron, but the iron in supplements, like your multivitamin is usually iron (II) fumarate ($C_4H_2FeO_4$), which is more easily absorbed by the blood stream than elemental iron.

- a magnet
- glassware you don't mind ruining
- and a source of heat, like a Bunsen burner or a stove top

First, combine the iron fillings and sulfur in a lab grade glass beaker or test tube, stirring them together. This is a mixture. The iron and sulfur are both still separate from one another. You can separate them back out by running the magnet along the bottom of the glassware. This will attract the iron filings to the magnet, separating them from the sulfur. You can see that the iron and sulfur aren't really combined. Now stir them together again and heat them over a Bunsen burner or a stove. The iron and sulfur will now chemically combine to make iron sulfide molecules.

These molecules are permanently bonded into molecules that we can't easily separate.

Let the mixture cool and throw it out along with your now ruined glassware.

### ☺ ☻ EXPERIMENT: There's Metal In My Cereal!

Most breakfast cereals are iron fortified with elemental or "reduced" iron so grab your favorite box of sugar coco balls and find the element iron.

1. Pour about a cup of cereal into a blender.
2. Cover with water.
3. Blend until smooth.
4. Now pour the whole thing out into a clear glass bowl. Use a magnet around the bottom edges of the bowl to attract the iron bits and collect them in one place.

Iron is an element. It is made up of only one type of atom, iron atoms.

### ☺ ☻ ☻ EXPERIMENT: Diapers

Baby diapers contain polyacrylic acid, a super-absorbent polymer. It's a powder that is mixed in with the fluff inside of the diaper. It is hydrophilic (loves water) because the carboylic acid groups (COOH) in the polymer can hydrogen bond to water molecules. Lay out a garbage bag on the table and tear open a clean baby diaper, removing the fluff. Collect the white powder you see. Spoon the powder into a cup and add water. Stir and watch what happens. What you see is two molecules, water and polyacrylic acid bonding together.

# THE ARTS: COLOR AND VALUE

Color is just light reflected off of objects. Objects all on their own aren't really any color at all. Instead, they get their color because of their ability to reflect a certain wavelength back to our eyes. In fact, objects can look like very different colors depending on the light they are in. Think of the surface of a lake or the ocean. In some lights it can look dull gray while at other times it may be striking turquoise, vivid blue, or green on the very same beach. Within artwork, color is very important because it is the main communicator of feeling within the art. Imagine the different feeling a painting of a beach would have if it were done in dingy blue gray shades versus bright, vivid turquoise shades.

## Additional Layer

The first scientist of color was Isaac Newton who wrote about color in *Optics* (1704). It was partly because of Newton's work with prisms that we came to call red, yellow, and blue the primary colors.

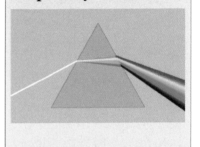

*The Bedroom At Arles by Van Gogh (c. 1889-90). The violets and blues of the walls harmonize with the green on the windows and walls and contrast with the yellows and reds of the furniture.*

## Additional Layer

Leonardo Da Vinci was one of the first artists to write about the curiosities of color. He said, "*The variety of color in objects cannot be discerned at a great distance, excepting in those parts which are directly lighted up by the solar rays.*"

Go outside on a sunny day and observe colors closely to see if this is true. What else do you observe about the colors you see. One of the keys to Leonardo's genius as an artist was his powers of observing closely. Practice this.

Color and value play a pivotal role in the feeling a piece of artwork portrays. There has been an incredible amount of research done on how humans respond to various shades and hues. Interestingly enough, scientists have discovered some science within the art of color. Most people have similar responses to certain colors. Blue is calming and soothing while red is energetic and active. Green promotes relaxation while yellow encourages quickness. Colors play a role in how we feel, how we think, and our reactions to situations, and also to art.

## Additional Layer

Rainbows are created out of white light splitting into colors as the light passes through raindrops, which act as prisms. Rainbows contain a continuous spectrum of all colors, but our eye picks out the primary and secondary colors.

## Fabulous Fact

In fact, the so-called primary colors are somewhat arbitrary. Why 3? Because humans have 3 different types of color receptors in our eyes and we perceive color in three parts. Why red, yellow, and blue? Partly because of rainbows and prisms and Newton and partly just because it is convention, even though not all colors can be mixed using these three. This is why printers use magenta, cyan, and yellow instead of red, yellow and blue.

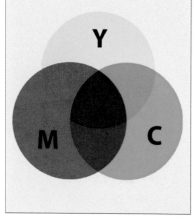

Color has three distinct characteristics:
- Hue is the the name of the basic color (red, orange, yellow, green, blue, or purple)
- Value is how light or dark it is
- Intensity is the brightness or dullness

Colors can also be described as warm (reds, oranges, yellows) or cool (blues, greens, purples). Of course, the basic hues can be combined an infinite number of ways, and can also be combined with black and white, to create all the different colors that make up our world.

## ☺ ☺ ☻ EXPLORATION: Hues on the Color Wheel

Hue refers to the actual color on the color wheel. There are 6 hues on the color wheel—red, orange, yellow, green, blue, and purple. Three of these are primary colors- red, yellow, and blue. Primary means first. The primary colors are the first colors, the colors that you cannot create by combining other colors. The secondary colors are created by combining the primary colors together. Tertiary colors are created by combining the secondary colors.

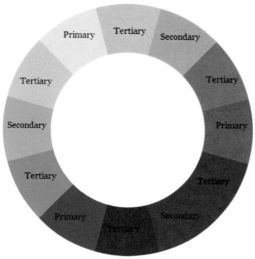

Use primary colored paints to create secondary and tertiary colors on a color wheel. You'll have to combine the primary colors to create the other hues. You'll find a printable to use at the end of the unit.

## ☺ ☺ ☻ EXPLORATION: Tints and Shades

Tints are created by combining hues with varying amounts of white. For example, red and white combine to create pink, a tint of red. Shades are created by combining hues with black. Navy blue is a shade of blue created by combining blue and black.

Combine each hue with black to create the shades and white to create the tints.

*Different tints and shades of the same hue of red.*

## ☺ EXPLORATION: Color Mixing for Tots
Gather these items: 3 glasses or jars of water, 3 empty glasses or jars, food coloring. Artists often start with basic colors on their palettes and then mix and combine them to create the various colors they want to use. Start by putting food coloring in each of the 3 glasses – one red, one blue, and one yellow. Now see what happens when you mix a little red and yellow together. Now mix a little yellow and blue. What do you get? Now try blue and red.

## ☺ ☺ ☺ EXPLORATION: Wax Resist
Review the color wheel and discuss which colors are warm and which are cool. Choose either warm or cool crayons and draw a quick picture, pressing hard with the crayons. When you're finished, paint over the drawing with thin, black tempera paint. The wax will resist the crayon.

Instead of using black paint, you may want to choose a color that

### Additional Layer
Your culture makes a difference in how you view colors. For example, the Chinese see blue and green as different shades of the same color. The Russians distinguish between blue and azure, but in English they're the same color. In Hungary dark red and bright red are viewed as completely separate colors with different basic words to describe them. And if you speak English you think of pink and red as completely different colors while you think of a saturated yellow and light yellow as the same basic color. Unless you live in my house of all boys where the occasional pink item that comes along is always referred to as "light red" for the sensitive sensibilities of my boys.

### Orange or Orange?
No one knows which word came first: the color orange or the fruit orange.

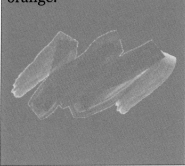

## Additional Layer
The photographs by Ansel Adams are beautiful examples of achromatic art:

*The Tetons and the Snake River, 1942*

## Paint Chip Namers
Check out the names on the paint chips in the store. Part of the name is usually a basic color word like "brown" or "red" or "yellow". The other part of the name is usually something designed to elicit an emotion in you. Sometimes the paint chip namers skip the color word and go straight for the heart, or the stomach as the case may be. My bedroom walls are "chocolate chip cookie dough" colored. Since colors and emotions are closely linked, this works.

goes with your theme and color scheme. For example, a cool underwater scene could be painted with blue. A cool mountain scene could be painted in purple. A warm desert scene could be painted in orange.

## ☺ ☻ EXPLORATION: Color Schemer
Color schemes are ways to combine colors that look harmonious to our eyes. Match each of these color schemes up with the painting done in that scheme. You may want to refer to a color wheel as you determine which is which.

| | |
|---|---|
| **Monochromatic:** Variations of one color made by mixing black or white with a particular hue |  *Paul Cezanne, Still Life With Onions* |
| **Analogous:** Composed of three colors that are neighbors on the color wheel |  *Pablo Picasso, The Tragedy* |
| **Complementary:** Made of two colors opposite each other on the color wheel. |  *Henri Rousseau, The Snake Charmer* |

Now have each person use oil pastels to create a picture using one of these color schemes. Begin by looking at a color wheel and selecting a scheme, then use only those colors to create a picture. Hang each picture up and have other kids try to guess which color scheme was used.

### ☺ ☻ ☻ EXPLORATION: Value

Value refers to the lightness or darkness of a color. Within every single hue there are a range of values, or tones. Use the value worksheet at the end of this unit and fill in each square with the color described. As you continue to mix the colors at 50% you will see how the tone lightens. This same concept can be repeated with a variety of hues. Combine a hue of your choice with either black or white and continue the progression.

Value can help artists show distance. The closest object in a painting is usually the darkest in value. As things get further away, the value lightens. This technique helps artists communicate distance and depth. You can see in this painting by Albert Bierstadt how he uses changing values in color to show distance.

*Yosemite by Albert Bierstadt*

### ☺ ☻ EXPLORATION: Achromatic Wildlife

Achromatic means free of color, or in other words-- black, white, or any shade of gray. These don't contain any particular hue. Pencil drawings, charcoals, and black and white photography are the most common achromatic arts. Do a pencil or charcoal sketch of a zebra as you talk about achromatic colors.

Go to www.DrawNow.com and search for "how to draw a zebra" for step-by-step instructions.

**Additional Layer**
The Impressionists were famous for playing with color. Look at these paintings by Monet, each of the same cathedral in Rouen, but in different light and therefore with different colors.

Monet did many more versions of this same cathedral in different lights. Look it up.

## Additional Layer

An after image occurs when your eye looks at one deeply saturated color for a long time. Once you look away your eye will still "see" the image, but in a complementary color.

Stare at the image for 30 seconds then look away at a white surface. You should see the correct colors.

## Writer's Workshop

Write about your favorite colors. What color is your bedroom painted? What color would I find most inside your closet?

## ☺ ☻ EXPLORATION: Color Me Happy

This chart shows some basic emotions that are elicited by colors.

| Red | Strong, active, passionate, aggressive, intense, raging, energetic, excited |
|---|---|
| Orange | Distressed, upset, daring, stimulating |
| Yellow | Cheerful, imaginative, intelligent, bright, wise |
| Green | Relaxed, natural, quiet, tranquil, tired, balanced, invigorated |
| Blue | Comfortable, secure, peaceful, calm, sad, lonely, down |
| Purple | Dignified, spiritual, calm, inspirational, associated with royalty |

Look through a home decorating magazine and find rooms decorated with some of these colors. Do the rooms match the feelings from the chart? Now look through an art book and find paintings done in some of the colors and discuss their emotions.

## ☺ ☻ ☻ EXPEDITION: Ketchup and Mustard

Drive around town and take note of the colors of the fast food signs you see. What colors do you find most often? Their décor, logos, signs, and food packaging are most predominantly two colors: red and yellow. Take a look at the responses people have to those colors. Why do you think a fast food chain would want to elicit that kind of response from its customers? Go pick up a variety of paint chips and design an appropriate color scheme for these businesses based on peoples' responses to colors: gas station, laundromat, grocery store, pet store, bowling alley, fancy restaurant, theater.

### Coming up next . . .

**Unit 1-13**

Ancient India
Grasslands – Elements
Texture & Form

**My Ideas For This Unit:**

Title: _____    Topic: _____

_____

_____

_____

_____

_____

_____

_____

_____

Title: _____    Topic: _____

_____

_____

_____

_____

_____

_____

_____

_____

_____

_____

Title: _____    Topic: _____

_____

_____

_____

_____

_____

_____

_____

_____

_____

**My Ideas For This Unit:**

Title: _____     Topic: _____

_____

_____

_____

_____

_____

_____

_____

_____

Title: _____     Topic: _____

_____

_____

_____

_____

_____

_____

_____

_____

_____

Title: _____     Topic: _____

_____

_____

_____

_____

_____

_____

_____

_____

_____

# Bedouin Travelers

Ancient Bedouins were nomadic. They traveled from place to place herding, fishing, transporting people and goods, and farming when they could. They mostly moved around because there wasn't much water, and they followed where the most water was.

Often Bedouin families traveled together. Family units were their most important division and loyalty was highly valued. Bedouins also valued honor. Sharaf was the name of their honor code. Telling the truth was so important that they had a special ritual for determining if someone was lying. It was called Bisha, or trial by fire, and involved licking a very hot object three times. If the accused had a burnt tongue from it, they had been lying according to the Bisha ceremony.

# Ancient Arabia: Unit 1-12

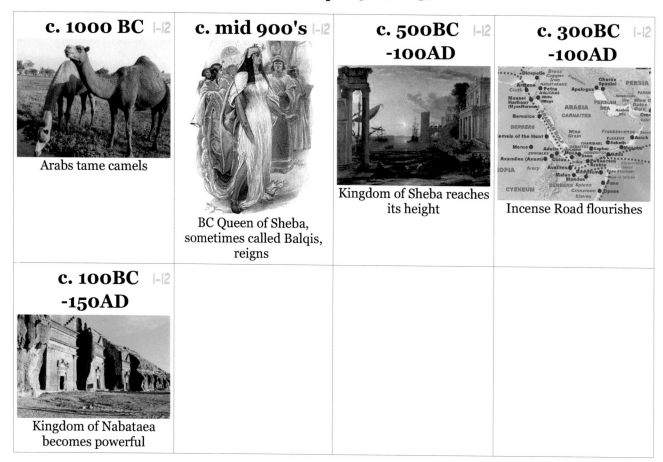

**c. 1000 BC** 1-12

Arabs tame camels

**c. mid 900's** 1-12

BC Queen of Sheba, sometimes called Balqis, reigns

**c. 500BC -100AD** 1-12

Kingdom of Sheba reaches its height

**c. 300BC -100AD** 1-12

Incense Road flourishes

**c. 100BC -150AD** 1-12

Kingdom of Nabataea becomes powerful

# Ancient Arabia

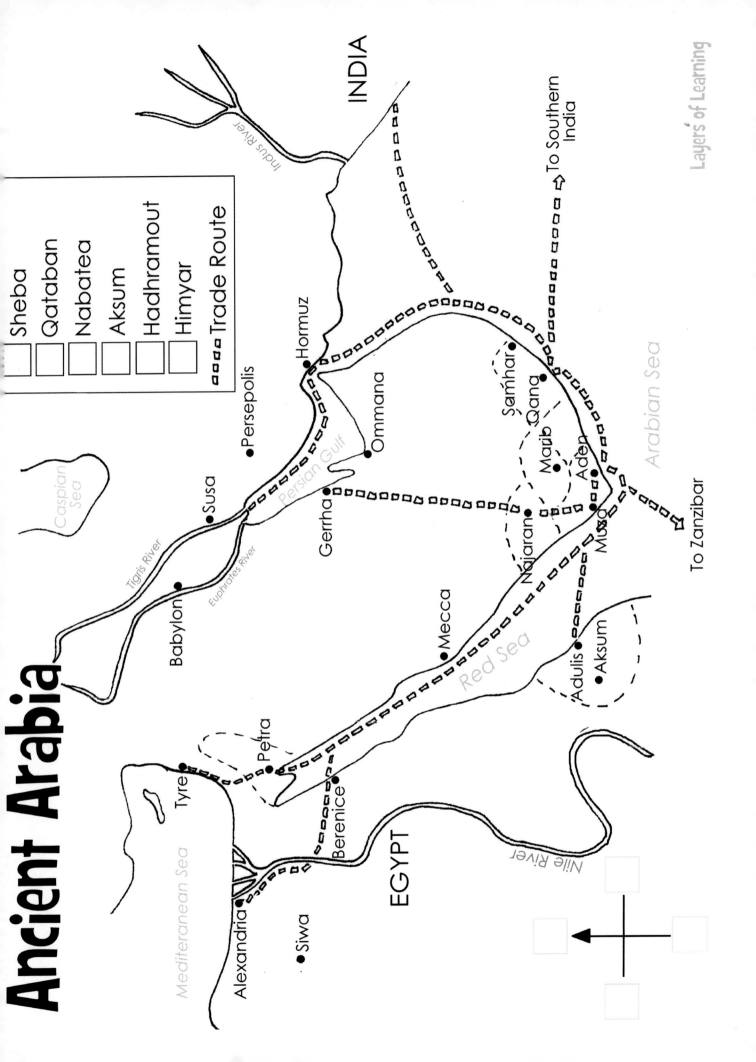

Sheba
Qataban
Nabatea
Aksum
Hadhramout
Himyar
Trade Route

Caspian Sea

INDIA

Indus River

Tigris River

Euphrates River

Persian Gulf

Babylon

Susa

Persepolis

Hormuz

Ommana

Gerrha

Şamhar
Qana
Marib
Najaran
Muza
Aden

To Southern India

Arabian Sea

Mecca

Red Sea

Adulis
Aksum

To Zanzibar

Petra

Tyre

Berenice

Alexandria

Siwa

Mediterranean Sea

Nile River

EGYPT

Layers of Learning

# Rivers of the World

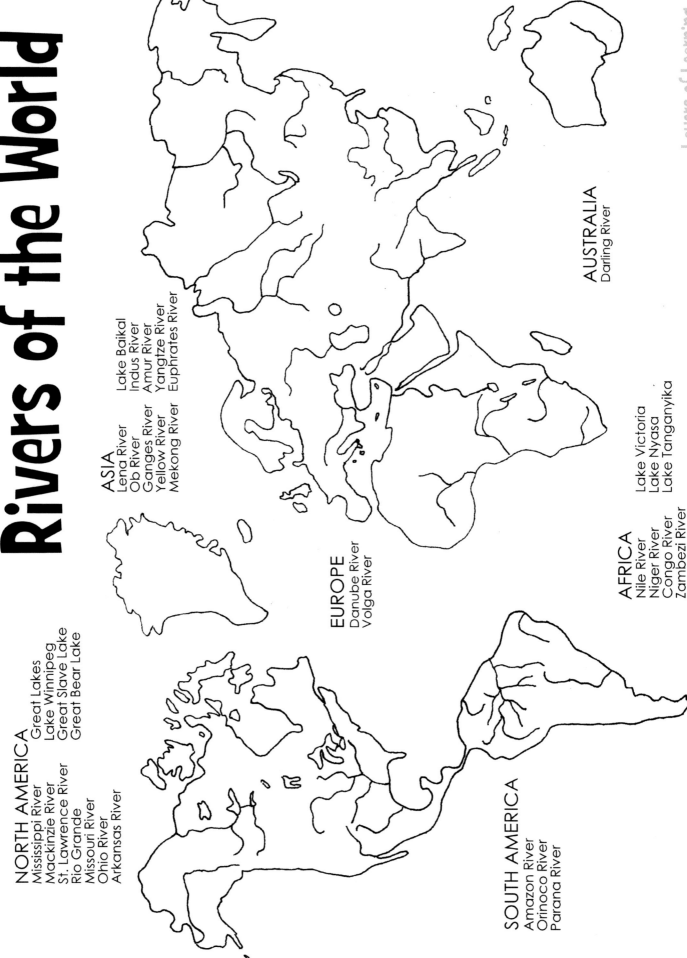

**NORTH AMERICA**
Mississippi River
Mackinzie River
St. Lawrence River
Rio Grande
Missouri River
Ohio River
Arkansas River
Great Lakes
Lake Winnipeg
Great Slave Lake
Great Bear Lake

**SOUTH AMERICA**
Amazon River
Orinoco River
Parana River

**ASIA**
Lena River
Ob River
Ganges River
Yellow River
Mekong River
Lake Baikal
Indus River
Amur River
Yangtze River
Euphrates River

**EUROPE**
Danube River
Volga River

**AFRICA**
Nile River
Niger River
Congo River
Zambezi River
Orange River
Lake Victoria
Lake Nyasa
Lake Tanganyika

**AUSTRALIA**
Darling River

# River Stages: Erosion, Transport, Deposition

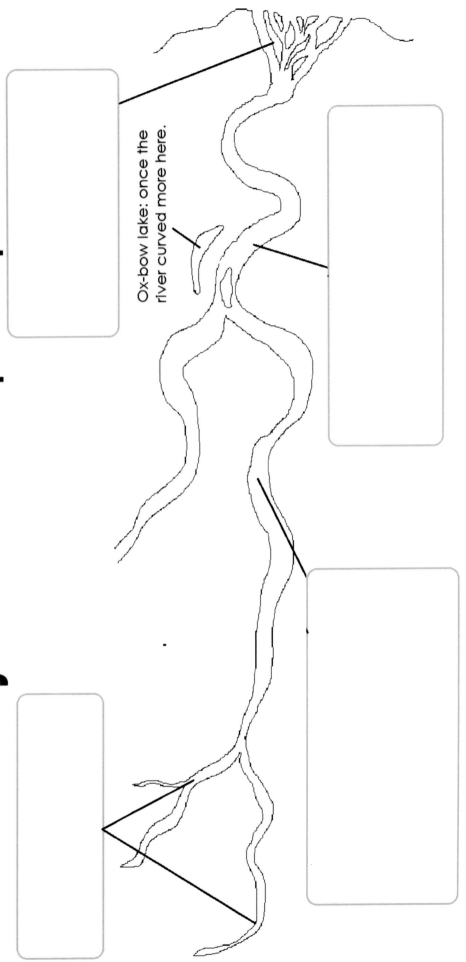

Ox-bow lake: once the river curved more here.

An older, slower river meanders slowly, depositing sediment on the upstream side of curves and wearing away banks.

A river in the middle courses carries a lot of sediment with it. It begins to deposit sediment on near banks and sometimes on the upstream side of blockages or slow spots, forming islands.

A young river, near the source, flows quickly and erodes the land

At the end of the river, many islands of deposits are sometimes formed creating a delta.

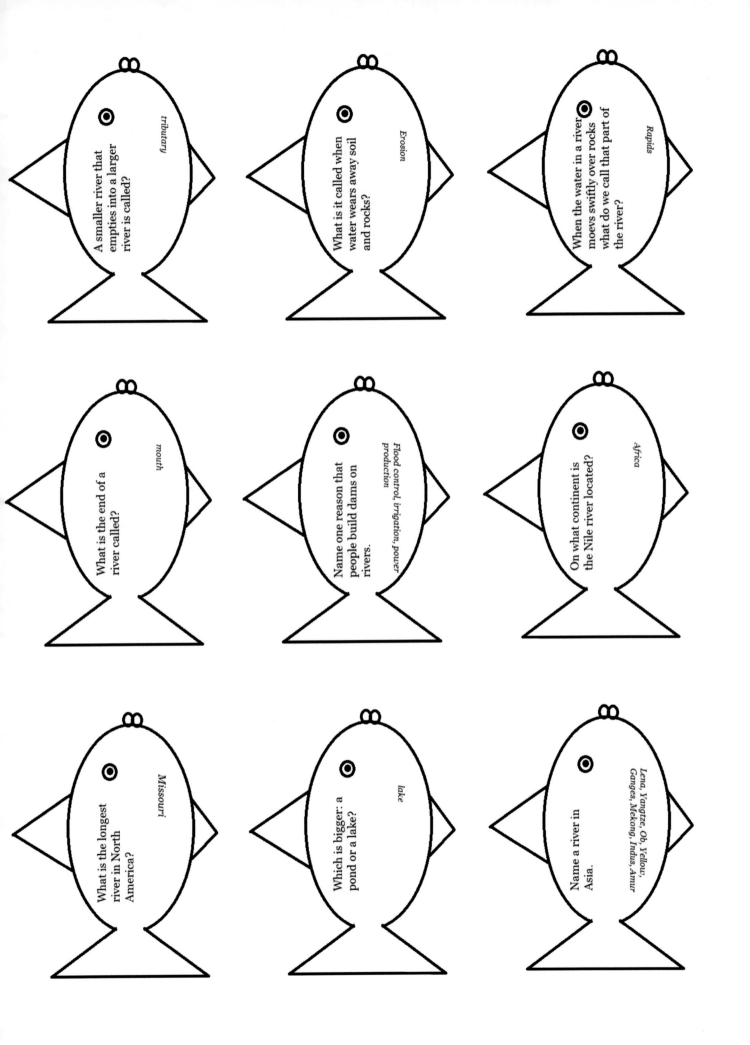

A smaller river that empties into a larger river is called?

*tributary*

What is it called when water wears away soil and rocks?

*Erosion*

When the water in a river moevs swiftly over rocks what do we call that part of the river?

*Rapids*

What is the end of a river called?

*mouth*

Name one reason that people build dams on rivers.

*Flood control, irrigation, power production*

On what continent is the Nile river located?

*Africa*

What is the longest river in North America?

*Missouri*

Which is bigger: a pond or a lake?

*lake*

Name a river in Asia.

*Lena, Yangtze, Ob, Yellow, Ganges, Mekong, Indus, Amur*

# Electron Structure

## S orbital

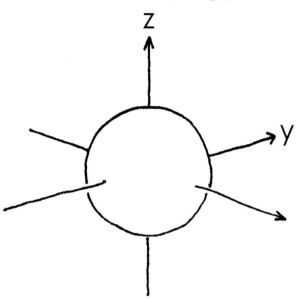

## P orbital

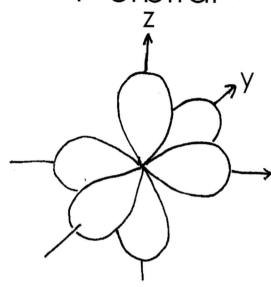

Each orbital contains how many electrons? _____

## D orbital

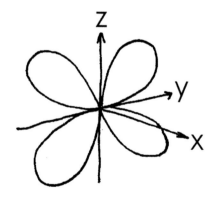
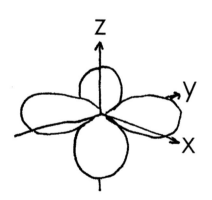
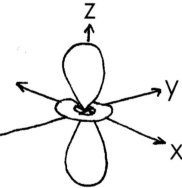

The D orbital is shown in three parts, but really they exist all together. It's broken up so you can see it properly.

F orbitals are incredibly complicated and messy, so we're not showing them.

# Filling the Electron Shells

Electrons always move to the place of lowest energy, closest to the nucleus. This chart shows the order in which electrons fill the orbitals around an atom. Start at the top. 1s, then 2s, 2p, 3s, 3p, 4s, 3d, 4p, 5s, 4d, 5p, 6s, 4f, 5d, 6p, 7s, 5f, and 6d. No stable atoms are larger than a 6d energy level so there we will stop.

1s

2s    2p

3s    3p    3d

4s    4p    4d    4f

5s    5p    5d    5f

6s    6p    6d

7s

Each of the circles on this sheet represents one orbital. Each orbital can hold two electrons. The electrons don't want to share if they don't have to so they will always fill one orbital each on a sub-shell until there are enough electrons that they have to share.

How many electrons can an s orbital hold? _____
How many electrons can a p orbital hold? _____
How many electrons can a d orbital hold? _____
How many electrons can an f orbital hold? _____

The element Iodine has 53 electrons. If I put two electrons each in orbitals until all 53 electrons are used up I could see which shells the electrons in Iodine are occupying. Chemists have a way of writing down the way an element fills its shells and orbitals.

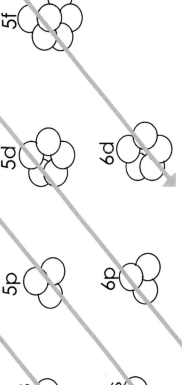

2nd shell — 2p$^6$ — 6 electrons in the orbital

p sub-shell

Here is the notation for Iodine:
$1s^2\ 2s^2\ 2p^6\ 3s^2\ 3p^6\ 4s^2\ 3d^{10}\ 4p^6\ 5s^2\ 4d^{10}\ 5p^5$

And here is another way to show where the electrons fall in Iodine:

1s ⇅  2s ⇅  2p ⇅⇅⇅  3s ⇅  3p ⇅⇅⇅  4s ⇅  3d ⇅⇅⇅⇅⇅

4p ⇅⇅⇅  5s ⇅  4d ⇅⇅⇅⇅⇅  5p ⇅⇅↑

Each arrow represents an electron. Electrons have a "spin", so one is shown with an up arrow and the other is shown with a down arrow. The only unpaired electron is the last one in the 5p orbital.

Carbon has 6 electrons. Write the notation and draw the arrow notation for Carbon.

Magnesium has 12 electrons. Write the notation and draw the arrow notation for Magnesium.

Iron has 26 electrons. Write the notation and draw the arrow notation for Iron.

# Filling the Electron Shells

Electrons always move to the place of lowest energy, closest to the nucleus. This chart shows the order in which electrons fill the orbitals around an atom. Start at the top, 1s, then 2s, 2p, 3s, 3p, 4s, 3d, 4p, 5s, 4d, 5p, 6s, 4f, 5d, 6p, 7s, 5f, and 6d. No stable atoms are larger than a 6d energy level so there we will stop.

How many electrons can an s orbital hold? __2__
How many electrons can a p orbital hold? __6__
How many electrons can a d orbital hold? __10__
How many electrons can an f orbital hold? __14__

The element Iodine has 53 electrons. If I put two electrons each in orbitals until all 53 electrons are used up I could see which shells the electrons in Iodine are occupying. Chemists have a way of writing down the way an element fills its shells and orbitals.

$2p^6$  — 6 electrons in the orbital
2nd shell
p sub-shell

Here is the notation for Iodine:
$1s^2\ 2s^2\ 2p^6\ 3s^2\ 3p^6\ 4s^2\ 3d^{10}\ 4p^6\ 5s^2\ 4d^{10}\ 5p^5$

And here is another way to show where the electrons fall in Iodine:

1s ⇅ 2s ⇅ 2p ⇅⇅⇅ 3s ⇅ 3p ⇅⇅⇅ 4s ⇅ 3d ⇅⇅⇅⇅⇅
4p ⇅⇅⇅ 5s ⇅ 4d ⇅⇅⇅⇅⇅ 5p ⇅⇅↑

Each arrow represents an electron. Electrons have a "spin", so one is shown with an up arrow and the other is shown with a down arrow. The only unpaired electron is the last one in the 5p orbital.

Carbon has 6 electrons. Write the notation and draw the arrow notation for Carbon. $1s^2\,2s^2\,2p^2$

1s ⇅  2s ⇅  2p ↑ ↑ ☐

Magnesium has 12 electrons. Write the notation and draw the arrow notation for Magnesium.
$1s^2\ 2s^2\ 2p^6\ 3s^2$

1s ⇅  2s ⇅  2p  ⇅⇅⇅  3s  ⇅

Iron has 26 electrons. Write the notation and draw the arrow notation for Iron. $1s^2\ 2s^2\ 2p^6\ 3s^2\ 3p^6\ 4s^2\ 3d^6$

1s ⇅  2s ⇅  2p  ⇅⇅⇅  3s ⇅  3p 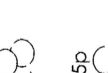 ⇅⇅⇅  4s  ⇅  3d  ⇅ ↑ ↑ ↑ ↑
3d ⇅ ↑ ↑ ↑ ↑

1s ◯

2s ◯◯◯

3s ◯◯◯

4s ◯◯◯

4f ◯◯◯◯◯◯◯

3d ◯◯◯◯◯

4d ◯◯◯◯◯

5d ◯◯◯◯◯

6d ◯◯◯◯◯

5f ◯◯◯◯◯◯◯

5s ◯◯◯

6s ◯◯◯

7s ◯

Each of the circles on this sheet represents one orbital. Each orbital can hold two electrons. The electrons don't want to share if they don't have to so they will always fill one orbital each on a sub-shell until there are enough electrons that they have to share.

# Timeline of the Discovery of the Atom Figures

## Rutherford's Atom

## Neutrons

## Electrons

## Electron Cloud

## Periods of Atoms

| I | II | III | IV | V |
|---|----|-----|----|----|
| Li | Be | B | C | N |
| Na | Mg | Al | Si | |

## Bohr's Atom

## Atom

## Protons
= Atomic Number

$Li^3$

# Color Wheel

Fill in this color wheel. Start by painting the primary colors in the center ring – red, yellow and blue. Now you'll paint the secondary colors in the middle ring. Where red and blue intersect, mix red and blue on your paint tray and paint it in that section, etc. Now continue to paint the tertiary colors in the outer ring.

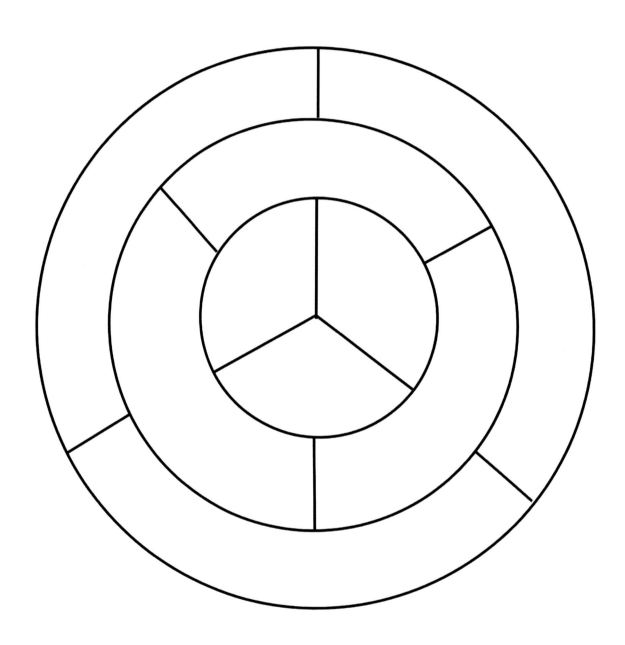

# Color Values

Choose 3 colors and paint the top square of each column with each color.
Now mix each with either 50% white or 50% black and paint that into the next box.
Continue to fill the boxes using the 50% rule as you work down.

# ABOUT THE AUTHORS

Karen & Michelle . . .
Mothers, sisters, teachers, women who are passionate
about educating kids.
We are dedicated to lifelong learning.

Karen, a mother of four, who has homeschooled her kids for more than eight years with her husband, Bob, has a bachelor's degree in child development with an emphasis in education. She lives in Utah where she gardens, teaches piano, and plays an excruciating number of board games with her kids. Karen is our resident Arts expert and English guru {most necessary as Michelle regularly and carelessly mangles the English language and occasionally steps over the bounds of polite society}.

Michelle and her husband, Cameron, homeschooling now for over a decade, teach their six boys on their ten acres in beautiful Idaho country. Michelle earned a bachelors in biology, making her the resident Science expert, though she is mocked by her friends for being the *Botanist with the Black Thumb of Death*. She also is the go-to for History and Government. She believes in staying up late, hot chocolate, and a no whining policy. We both pitch in on Geography, in case you were wondering, and are on a continual quest for knowledge.

*Visit our constantly updated blog for tons of free ideas,*
*free printables, and more cool stuff for sale:*
www.Layers-of-Learning.com

Made in the USA
Monee, IL
06 August 2020